DREAM MORE

www.**transworldbooks**.co.uk

DREAM MORE

MORE

CELEBRATE

THE DREAMER

IN YOU

Dolly Parton

BANTAM PRESS

LONDON • TORONTO • SYDNEY • AUCKLAND • JOHANNESBURG

TRANSWORLD PUBLISHERS
61–63 Uxbridge Road, London W5 5SA
A Random House Group Company
www.transworldbooks.co.uk

First published in Great Britain
in 2012 by Bantam Press
an imprint of Transworld Publishers

A CIP catalogue record for this book
is available from the British Library.

ISBN 9780593071816

Book design by Meighan Cavanaugh

The author gratefully acknowledges permission to reprint the following:
page 2: © Fran Strine. Reprinted with permission; *page 12*: © AP Photo/
M. Spencer Green. Reprinted with permission; *page 28*: © shaunf
lanneryphotography.com. Reprinted with permission; *page 58*: © SDPros.co.
Reprinted with permission; *page 80*: © Gary Woods and the Robert F.
Thomas Foundation. Reprinted with permission; *page 102*: © Laura Eady.
Reprinted with permission; *page 110*: © photo courtesy of Dollywood
Publicity. Reprinted with permission.

Addresses for Random House Group Ltd companies outside the UK
can be found at: www.randomhouse.co.uk
The Random House Group Ltd Reg. No. 954009

The Random House Group Limited supports the Forest Stewardship
Council (FSC®), the leading international forest-certification organization.
Our books carrying the FSC label are printed on FSC®-certified paper. FSC
is the only forest-certification scheme endorsed by the leading environmental
organizations, including Greenpeace. Our paper procurement policy can be
found at www.randomhouse.co.uk/environment.

Typeset in Adobe Caslon Pro
Printed and bound in Great Britain by
CPI Group (UK) Ltd, Croydon, CR0 4YY

2 4 6 8 10 9 7 5 3 1

*I dedicate this book to all of the people who have helped
me with my Imagination Library and believe as I do
that reading is the fuel for a child's imagination.*

*I especially want to acknowledge David Dotson
for his leadership of my Dollywood Foundation
and Imagination Library and for spreading
my dreams for children across the United States,
Canada, and the United Kingdom.*

*Finally, this book is for my Daddy, who never learned
to read and write, and paid a dear price for that,
and inspired me to not let it happen to others.*

PREFACE

I refuse to settle for something less than great. And if it takes a lifetime, then that's how long I'll wait. 'Cause all I want is everything . . . is that too much to ask?

I peeked through the black curtain to see the audience, just the way I had done a thousand times before. No matter how many times you appear in front of an audience, there is a compulsive need to see just what they look like before you jump out onstage. After all these years, I know that every audience is different, but they're always familiar, too, as many of my great fans and folks who have followed my career since the early days will be there.

But this audience was different, remarkably different. There were nearly ten thousand of them and almost all were in their early twenties. This was the University of Tennessee graduating class, and the university had invited me to give the commencement speech. The trustees also planned to bestow an honorary doctorate on me at the end of the ceremony. I was about to become Dr. Dolly.

As I looked out at all those young, energetic faces, I couldn't help but drift into a realm of wonder. I wondered: If my husband, Carl Dean, and I had had a baby girl, would she have graduated from here? What would her dreams be? A singer, a model, a businesswoman? What would she look like? Blond, full-figured, skinny, fat? Would we have been good parents with my being on the road all the time? How would Carl have handled all that?

What about a boy? A Dolly Parton boy! I can't imagine. A tall, dark, handsome fellow like his dad? Or a drag queen? Oh, my stars.

Then suddenly the reality hit me. I had accepted an invitation to give a speech in less than thirty minutes that was to inspire young people, when their parents and teachers had had more than twenty years to influence them. Whatever had made me think I could do this?

Over the years, I have talked with lots of groups of kids. I've always known I could relate to them, but this wasn't the same. This wasn't about relating or entertaining; this was about whether I had the ability to say something that might make a difference in their futures.

I had spent hours preparing my speech. But would the jokes and thoughts that I had about what was important to say mean anything to these college graduates on this day?

I glanced up from the back of the stage, and there was Chancellor Jimmy Cheek of the University of Tennessee and the governor at that time, Phil Bredesen, who had become a very good friend of mine during his administration. Both of them were going to speak before I did. Such respected and educated public speakers would surely say all the right things. And if they said all the right things, what would be left for me to say? Would my speech just be redundant?

Oh, please, Lord. I have to quit this second-guessing. I will just have to go out there and speak from my heart and tell everybody some things I've learned from all my years of experience. Surely there must be a gem or two in my own life that will benefit some of them.

During the ceremony, it turned out that other people had a lot to say. As I stood in the wings waiting to go onstage, I thought the academic speeches would never end. But when the governor finally introduced me, he said such nice things about how he and others were inspired by some of the things I had done that his words gave me the focus I needed. I realized I should just share some of my inner self with those kids.

There were parents and teachers in the audience, but mostly students. And when I hit the stage, they all sprang to their feet. What a warm welcome and what a relief. *I can do this*, I thought to myself as I looked out at them clapping and cheering.

In preparing my speech, I had decided to use four principles that guide our mission at my Dollywood Foundation for the Imagination Library. In our foundation work, we talk about the values we would like to instill in children from birth to kindergarten and beyond.

As I reviewed these four guiding points, I discovered that they really apply to all people of all ages. We are simply saying in our foundation that these ideas should start when children are small. In fact, I believe that if you get it right with children when they're young, then it becomes a part of their character for life. So I wrote a speech about these ideals and I delivered it from my heart.

When I finished speaking, I received a standing ovation. I can honestly say it was the most rewarding applause that I've ever received.

As I wrote this book, I reviewed that speech over and over. No matter how many accolades I received for it, I felt I did not say everything that I could or should have said. Probably, if I had made a longer speech, people in the audience would have walked out or started texting their friends, saying, "I wish she'd shut up so we can go party." This book covers more of what I wish I had said.

Whatever your station in life, I hope you glean something from this little book that inspires you to *dream* of doing more with your life, *learn* from everything you see and do, *care* for everyone and everything that crosses your path, and *be more* than you ever dreamed you could become.

There's a star in all of us,
We're all diamonds in the rough.
We're little engines chuggin' down the line.
There are dreams we hold inside
Waitin' till the time is right.
So keep the faith, you'll have your time
    to shine.

Let nobody block your path,
Allow nothing to distract
The passion and desire inside your heart.
There is nothing you can't do,
There's no dream that can't come true
With faith and love and trust enough to start.
So celebrate the dreamer in you.
Only you can make it come true.
Dream more, learn more, care and be more;
Wishes do come true.
Celebrate the dreamer in you.

One

DREAM MORE

The magic is inside you . . . there ain't no crystal ball.

down, regret, or clue, a dream that
with desires of candy and cash, when our
were sweet thoughts, until she [...] until [...]
Dreams took me into the [...] of the foothills
of the Great Smoky Mountains, between [...]

*D*on't ask me how I feel about dreaming unless you really have some time to listen.

Since my early childhood, I've felt like my dreams were the foundation of my drive to accomplish all the things I love. It was a dream that made me feel dressed up when I just had old hand-me-down, ragged clothes. A dream that filled me up with desserts of candy and cake when all we had were sweet thoughts, cornbread and molasses.

Dreams took me from a shack at the foothills of the Great Smoky Mountains to Nashville and then to Hollywood. And then around the world, like Cinderella and the Fairy Godmother all combined, in glitter, high heels and hair.

It's a long way from the foothills of the Smoky Mountains to the top of the world, but I'm here—much to my delight and thanks to the love and support of many fine people. I don't take any of it or them for granted. I know that I am living the all-American dream. But chasing your dreams happens everywhere and there are dreamers like me all over the world. It makes me proud and humble to hear them say that my life has inspired them in some way.

While I'm proud of what I've done, the older I get, the more humble I feel. Yes, I've worked hard. Yes, I've been lucky. And yes, I've been truly blessed. But I always count my blessings far more than I ever count my money.

I asked my mother once why she thought God let me be so successful and didn't give the same opportunities to many of my family when some of them were far more talented than I am. She said, "God has his purpose for everybody. We all have our journey to walk." And she said she thought God knew that I'd be willing to share. Well, I always pray that I have enough to share and some to spare. And so far, God has obliged me.

I still struggle with how to help my kinfolks be more successful in music, and I suffer sometimes from a guilt complex about my own success, feeling that so many of them are so deserving. But I ask God to lead and to direct us all and to just let me be there when I'm needed, if I'm needed and as I'm needed. And I pray their dreams will eventually all come true.

I always dreamed hard and had a big imagination. When I was a kid, I used to put a tin can on a tobacco stick. I would jab one end of it into a crack on the porch of our old cabin. And those were not chickens out there in the yard, they were my audience. And that was no ragged dress I was wearing, it was a dress all aglitter with rhinestones. And it was made of the finest silk. Of course, in my mind's eye, I was standing onstage with my guitar and singing my heart out into a microphone, with thousands of people listening to me.

It was all a dream, but it was a dream that I just couldn't get enough of. I've held on to the dream every day of my life ever since and done everything I could to make it come true. I learned early on that I could get a lot of attention, especially from my Uncle Bill, by singing and writing little songs. And my Uncle Bill has been there with me all along.

> *I was gonna be rich no matter how much*
>   *it cost.*
> *I 'uz gonna win no matter how much I lost.*
> *All through the years I've kept my eye on*
>   *the prize.*
> *And yes, it's been worth the sacrifice.*

The night I graduated from Sevier County High School back in 1964, all the graduates had been asked to stand up and talk about what we were going to do with the rest of our lives. Everybody had a different story. Some said they were going to get married. Others said they were going to take a job in Knoxville. When it came my time, I stood up and said, "I'm going to Nashville and I'm gonna be a star." Well, the whole place laughed out loud. I was so embarrassed. *Why is everybody laughing?* I thought. *That is exactly what I want to do.* I felt they were being really cruel. But as bad as I felt and as embarrassed as I was, that moment did not shake me from my dreams. I knew what I needed to do to make my dream come true.

The passing of the years gives you a clearer perspective, so now I really don't think the people were laughing to be cruel or making fun of me. They were just not used to someone dreaming that big or being that sure about it. I always believe that people with big dreams don't often announce them because if they fail, the whole world knows.

I'm sure you've heard someone accuse another person of being a dreamer. Unfortunately, the term "dreamer" is frequently associated with laziness or with people who wish they could do something but who aren't willing to get off their assets and put them to work.

A dream can be a nightmare if you let it turn into one. If you just sleepwalk through this world, you're never going to accomplish anything. And the cold, hard facts are that not every dream comes true and not everything you touch turns to gold. But sometimes a failure is just a success dressed in different clothes.

Of course, you have to be careful. Do not confuse dreams with wishes. There is a difference. Dreams are where you visualize yourself being successful at what's important to you to accomplish. And dreams build convictions. Because you work hard to pay the price to make sure that they come true. Wishes are hoping that good things will happen to you. With wishes, there is no fire in your gut, pushing you to the limit to overcome every obstacle to reach your heart's desire. My desire to pursue my dreams has always been greater than my fear of not accomplishing them.

I thank God for my failures. Maybe not at the time, but after some reflection. I never feel like a failure just because something I tried has failed. To me, the secret is all in how you approach things.

Attitude, it's all an attitude.
Just because you fail, don't mean you have
    to lose.
But if you want to win, then here's the simple
    truth.
You have to change your attitude.

The truth is, I have done lots of projects that were less than successful. By some people's standards, they were okay. But they were sure not what I dreamed they could be.

I strive to do great things. Maybe that's what makes me work so hard and why some of the things I have done that have lived up to my dreams make up for the others that haven't. The dream that carried me from my mountain home to Nashville and beyond was to simply perform on the stage at the Grand Ole Opry. Growing up, that's pretty much all I talked about, all I thought about and all I dreamed about. So when that moment finally came, I knew then that no matter what else happened in my life—good and bad—I had fulfilled my greatest dream. Of course, I went on to dream more and I am thankful that I've had many more dreams come true. But just knowing that my first (and maybe my most special) dream came true always eases the disappointment that comes from dreams that don't turn out the way I envisioned.

In any event, I am my own worst critic and I

really try to learn from my mistakes. Sometimes I just don't talk about them. That sounds like a politician . . . brag about your successes and sweep your shortcomings under the rug. But thinking about what I did right and what I didn't do right helps me.

When things haven't gone well, it's very easy to start blaming others for what went wrong. Well, I'm human. I've done that, too. After all, I'm not perfect, even though I'd like to think my little nieces and nephews think so.

After time, however, I start thinking about why and what lesson God wanted me to learn from it. Usually he slaps me in the face with something so obvious that I feel stupid I hadn't seen it before. Then I realize he was pointing it out so that I would not make the same mistake on the next, even bigger project.

It seems that each project I take on is bigger and better than the last. (This does not include plastic surgery.) The key is to never be bitter. Bitterness is usually caused by holding on to something far longer than you need to. I have learned to let things go, as I truly believe all things happen for a reason and know that just because I want something to happen, it doesn't mean that it should happen or that it will.

So when something doesn't go my way or I stumble, I pick myself up, make sure I brush the disappointment off my rhinestones, and try not to harden my heart over it. Instead, I set about trying to strengthen the muscles around it.

Today I dream of making more movies, creating and producing more television shows, especially for children, and writing more children's books and music. I dream of writing my life story as a Broadway musical. I dream of my own cosmetics company. I dream of more Dollywoods and Dixie Stampedes. I dream that every child in the world will have an opportunity for their dreams to come true.

Of course, to make all this happen, I have to dream bigger; I have to work harder. And that is fine with me. I never will retire. And I hope I won't ever go to seed. As they say, I would certainly rather wear out than rust out. I hope that I drop dead right onstage one of these days, doing exactly what I want to do. It might shake up the audience a little bit, but I hope everybody knows that's exactly what I want. And I want people to simply walk around me and say, "Oh, just look at her. Is she smiling? She looks so happy, like she's having sweet dreams. I'm so glad we were with her when she went."

I just hope it doesn't happen today or tomorrow—but I know it will someday. And when it does, just know that I went happy, because chasing my dreams is what I do love to do. I want you to chase your dreams. So if I have but one wish for you, it is to *dream more*.

Dolly Parton

Just look around at those on top.
They held their dreams and never stopped.
Planted them in fertile fields
And watched them as they grew.
Little engines proud and bold,
Never faltered 'neath their load.
Saw their destination through
And you can, too.
So celebrate the dreamer in you.

Two

LEARN MORE

*You're not going to see your dreams
come true if you don't put wings,
legs, arms, hands and feet on 'em.*

Boy, did I not like school. I guess a lot of kids feel the same way. I'm still not sure what I learned in school, except that boys were a distraction. They still are. (Hey, I'm married, not blind!) Plus, it's hard to concentrate on history when you're dreaming about performing at the Grand Ole Opry.

In school I only made average grades. I have a couple of theories about why that was. My first grade school was a scary place for me. It was a one-room school with a teacher who taught first through eighth grade by himself. He was big and tall, with a real loud voice. And I was scared to death of him. He wasn't mean, but I started school a year early because my birthday was in January, so I was too young to know that he wasn't. He was pretty strict. He had to be, because some of those older country boys were pretty rambunctious. He didn't stand for any shenanigans.

I had never really been anywhere but home, so my first impression of school may have gotten me off to a bad start. Too young and too scared was a bad combination.

Whatever the real reason was, I know that I was smart. But at the time I wasn't smart enough to learn a lot from books, even though I liked to read. It took me a while to realize that the more you learn, the easier it is *to* learn. But I think it didn't really hit me until after school. Boy, did I learn a few things when I hit Nashville (but we'll save those for my *Dolly Does Nashville* book).

I thank God that when I was a kid, my Mama used to read the Bible to us. We didn't have television and our radio was used only to listen to the Grand Ole Opry each week and the news. So Mama was our entertainment. She sang, she read the Bible to us and she showed us how to cook and sew and make something out of nothing. And I'm still doing that.

The Bible was the only book we had in the house each and every day. I have such fond memories of sitting on Mama's lap, huddled near the warmth of the fire. The stories from the Old Testament were wild, vivid stories of good and bad that both scared and excited me. It made me want to know more, and most of all, it made me want to read more.

Today I read everything I can get my hands on. I believe that when you can read, even if you don't get a chance to get an education, you can truly learn about everything. I love historical fiction, fairy tales and books about religion and philosophy. But no matter what, if you give it to me, I'm gonna read it.

To me, reading is more than going on the Internet to learn how to fix my toaster. While that's helpful (though it might ruin my nails), I think reading is a much more emotional and creative experience.

When I'm all curled up and wrapped in my favorite blankets to read a book, it's as if the world does not exist to me. I read on two levels—one to absorb the content of the book (what the author is trying to say) and the other to absorb the author's creativity, which helps me to feel my own creativity.

I remain totally convinced that if we could do one simple thing to help kids and adults to learn more, it would be to inspire them to read more. I know it seems obvious and maybe dumb, but I have noticed that people I've met who love reading tend to be more engaged and more creative.

I really think my Dad inspired me to create my Imagination Library. He passed away in 2000. But before he died, we were visiting one day and he told me how proud he was of me. I asked him why and fully expected him to say something about *9 to 5* or "I Will Always Love You," or for sure the fact that I had become a member of the Grand Ole Opry and achieved the dream I'd had for years. But not at all. He was most proud of the fact that the kids around the county called me the Book Lady. This started early on, as the Imagination Library spread from my hometown to other communities—little children much too young to know me as a singer or a writer came to know me simply as the Book Lady. To them (and probably to you!), I look like some cartoon character who loves them so much that I figured out a way to help them have a roomful of books.

My Daddy never learned to read or write, but he was still very smart. I think from him I realized that learning comes easier if you can read.

But learning is really all about experience, how you look at everything you do and draw lessons from what you have done. If you learn from that and you don't make the same mistakes twice, then not only are you smart, you have what we call "horse sense." I believe in horse sense first and foremost. For those of you who don't know exactly what that means, it's just good ol' common sense that allows you to know what you need in any situation.

When I finally started to make some extra money and people in my hometown thought I was famous and earning even more than I really was, I decided it was time to live up to being a home-town celebrity. I started going home and giving concerts to raise money to buy band uniforms and instruments for my high school. After all, I had been in the high school band and I played drums.

In 1986, I started my Dollywood Company and the Dollywood Foundation. We got involved in the local schools and gave small scholarships to high school seniors interested in music and the environment. At the time, it seemed right and natural to do what I could to help the local school system. In fact, we had the superintendent of schools and that year's Tennessee teacher of the year on our foundation board.

In 1990, because we were giving scholarships to high school seniors, it became clear that nearly one-third of the kids in our local schools were not graduating—a 34 percent dropout rate. Research showed that most of them were making their minds up in the fifth and sixth grades that they didn't need to graduate to work on the farm or in the tourist business. Well, I knew better.

I remember being in the fifth and sixth grades. Those are the beginnings of raging hormones and when you become smarter than your parents and your teachers. So I invited all the fifth- and sixth-graders from Sevierville to Dollywood as my guests and held an assembly in our large theater at the Park. I think they thought I was going to be

doing a concert. I didn't, but we really did enter-
tain them. I committed to every one of them that
if they graduated from high school, I would pay
them each five hundred dollars. Each of them had
to select a buddy and keep him in school also. It
wasn't that much money, but it gave them in-
centive, knowing that somebody cared, that they
would and could learn more.

The program was a huge success. Not only did
it get the kids' attention, the parents, teachers and
the entire county got behind other programs to
make sure the kids made it. The dropout rate for
those classes was only 6 percent, and it remains
excellent to this day. Yet it also made me realize
that most kids just want to feel special and to know
that someone cares for them. The Buddy Program turned on a light for me, as it gave me a clear
direction for how I could help all children. My
mission became to find ways I could tell children
that there are people who care for them and love
them and, most of all, want them to learn more.

4-U are special in God's sight.
U are more than meets the eye.
So come on, get on with your life
And do it 4-U.

In the process of dealing with fifth- and sixth-graders, we learned that their problems and attitudes about school had started at the very beginning of school, in the first grade. We were determined to solve this problem, so we interviewed first-grade teachers. They told us the problem was that there were too many kids at different levels and not enough help to give the slower ones the personal time they needed. Well, guess what? The Dollywood Foundation paid for additional assistant teachers in every first-grade class for two years and assumed the school system would pay for it after that if it saw that the program really worked.

What we learned was heartbreaking and really hit home with me. The real problem turned out to be that some kids who entered first grade could already read and write and had a huge jump on the others. The others were not dumb or any different, really, except that their parents had not exposed them to reading or helped them to love reading and learning, because they believed that would be the teacher's role.

To compound the problem, the teachers would give gold stars to the ones who were ahead, making the others feel that something was wrong with them and that they were dumb. This system was destroying self-esteem at the very beginning of a child's life, when they most need reinforcement and encouragement. Boy, could I relate to that, having been raised poor in the hills, and remembering how many times "poor" had been mistaken for dumb or less important or beneath the richer kids.

The real truth was that education wasn't about being rich or poor. It was simply that some parents had done much more than others to get their kids prepared. Maybe some parents had to work two jobs, or maybe they just didn't care about helping their kids get a leg up. It makes no difference. All kids are special.

When I thought about my Mama reading the Bible to us, it hit me that if kids had books in the home, just maybe somebody would read to them and help them love books. Even more important, maybe it would inspire them and spark in them the kind of wild imagination that I have so they will thirst for what's out there in the big world.

So here's where everything I had learned in my efforts to help my hometown kids came together, in what I thought would be just another way for a local girl to help her community. We started a program in 1996 and we called it the Imagination Library. Our goal was to give every child in the county one book every month, mailed to their home and addressed to the child, from the day they were born until they were ready to start kindergarten. The books were free to all the kids. The foundation paid for the books in communities where I have a business like Dollywood, Dixie Stampede or Pirates Voyage. We have hundreds of great sponsors now all over the world, who help us in their communities.

This program started with two thousand books a month for local children. Now, much to my amazement, we have the program all across America, in Canada and in the United Kingdom. To date we have given away more than forty million books, and now we can visualize that the number someday will be forty billion.

If I'm remembered one hundred years from now, I hope it will be not for looks but for books. (I don't want to be responsible for any boobs in the future! I had to get that off my chest.)

No amount of money could buy from me
The memories that I have of then.
No amount of money could pay me
To go back and live through it again.
In the good ol' days when times
    were bad.

I learned all about hard work from my Daddy. By the time Mama and Daddy were in their mid-thirties, they had twelve kids to feed. He worked all the time, day and night, without ever thinking about a vacation or even a day off. (Not that he could afford to take one.) So whether this was passed on to me through his genes or by watching him, I've always had a strong work ethic. Now, I may go overboard sometimes by trying to do too much, but that's just me.

When I was asked to write music for a Broadway musical and the producers told me they needed fifteen songs, I wrote thirty. If I'm asked to do a media tour to promote a record and a tour, I will do thirty interviews in two days. When I'm at Dollywood to support the season's opening, I start at seven a.m. and end at nine p.m. every day while I'm there.

I'll never complain for one second about all that is expected of me, given my position, because it's written in Luke, "To whom much is given, much is expected." This is what I dreamed of and longed for my entire life. But it is work: some days are full of interviews, two hours of photos with Dollywood and Dixie Stampede employees, recording videos, greetings, shooting commercials, convening a planning meeting for our companies . . . and that is just on a Saturday.

I know that a good part of my work ethic comes from my desire to give the best that I can at all times. I never have considered myself a perfectionist, but I do think of myself as a "professionalist." I know that's not a real word, but I really can't think of a better way to describe my approach to work.

What I do know is that "perfectionist" means something different to everybody. But "professionalist" means that I always strive simply to be my very best.

A strong work ethic also has to do with my energy. I am asked all the time where I get my energy. I like to think of it as good, healthy energy that keeps me soaring past the obstacles and keeps me flying.

People think I am a vegan. . . . I'm not. Or they think I take lots of vitamins. . . . I don't. Or they think I have a daily exercise routine. But I certainly can't jog or I'd black both my eyes and beat myself to death. So where does all my energy come from? Well, I'm blessed that I do not require much sleep, which is a very good thing for me. For example, when I was writing this chapter, I had just finished six hours of interviews for the United Kingdom. There's a six-hour time difference between England and Nashville, so I started at two a.m. Nashville time so I could be on their morning shows. I like being awake to see and hear everything that goes on in life every second. God gave me a big break by not requiring me to sleep much.

He also gave me the blessing of being able to take power naps. Just let me close my eyes for even a few minutes, and I will wake up fresh and ready to go.

I've thought about this a lot, and I think that having lots of energy is mostly about having happiness in your life. And to me, happiness is your commitment to appreciating all that is good in life, big and small. It's pretty easy to be happy when everything's going great. But life's not like that. It's like one of my favorite old sayings goes, "If you want the rainbow, you have to put up with the rain."

To Me, If You're a Happy Person, You:

- Love what you do.
- Like yourself.
- Enjoy other people: their company, their ideas, their personalities.
- Keep a good spiritual grip on things.
- Always pray for understanding and acceptance.

Of course, I don't know if these account for your happiness, but they certainly account for mine. And it's been my experience that happiness begets happiness. You have to work hard at being happy, just like you have to work hard at being miserable. I wake up every day expecting all to be good and right. And if it's not, I set my mind to making it so by the end of the day. You just have to figure out where the unhappiness is coming from and then set about fixing it. In many ways, it's

what some couples say is the key to their relationship. They make a point to never go to bed mad at
each other. That's easy for me and Carl. I'm always gone.

It's easy to let your unhappiness sit there, just
like it's easy to let your anger sit there. But you
can't do that. You have to feel it and fix it.

You better get to livin', and
Don't forget to throw in a little forgivin'
And love along the way.
You better get to knowin',
Showin' a little bit more concern about where
you're goin'.
Just word unto the wise,
You better get to livin'.

I learned early on that if you can just get started
at doing something positive, somehow you are
starting on the downhill side of your problem.
When the big things in your life get messy, you

need to get up and get out. I make a point to appreciate all the little things in my life. I go out and smell the air after a good, hard rain. I re-read passages from my favorite books. I hold the little treasures that somebody special gave me. These small actions help remind me that there are so many great, glorious pieces of good in the world.

Writing is my therapy. It gives voice to my feelings. I often deal with my emotions by writing songs. Some are published and some are just personal feelings that I have. I realize this is not something that comes naturally to a lot of people, so I also feel a great joy knowing that as I work out my feelings in my songs, I may be helping you to give a voice to your feelings as well.

We all go through down times in our lives, myself included. People problems, female problems, male problems, family problems . . . you name it, I've felt it. Yet I'm glad I've been through those times. When they happen, you feel like it's God telling you to slow down and take inventory. We all need to know what it's like to be totally human, and, boy, do you feel totally human after those times. Those experiences also allow you to feel every human emotion and to sympathize and understand everybody.

When those times happen, I give myself an ultimatum. I tell myself, "You need to get off your self-pitying butt and get your misery out of everybody's face." People always say, "But you always look so happy." Well, that's Botox! Nobody's happy all the time. But I work hard at it.

I learned years ago to be around people who give me energy and stay away from people who drain energy from me. Everybody has both kinds of people in their lives. I call them energy vampires. They do not want to share your energy—they want to suck it out of you.

When you're young, you often misread these people. They seem to want to help; but after a while, you realize they are out to steal from you.

And I'm not talking so much about your money or your possessions, although that sometimes comes with the vampire. I'm talking about stealing your happiness, your well-being, even your personality and your creativity. There are some who can constantly put a monkey on your back. It is their monkey, but somehow you end up carrying it. Often they're people you really care for, but they constantly have problems that they want to share with you. And you are constantly trying to fix things for them. In truth, you worry more about their problems than you do your own. They can be friends, family or people you work with. I often accept it as my load, and I can carry more than most. However, I know now that I can give people everything they need but not everything they want. And to this day, I remain leery of monkeys.

Eventually, everyone figures out these people are bad for you. The trick is to learn it sooner than later. Then, once you do figure it out, to have the courage to acknowledge and fix it. I wish I could tell you what to look for, but it's different for everybody. All I can say is that the energy vampires I know have fangs and they show up in the daylight as well as at night. So I suggest you drive a stake right through the heart of the matter and get rid of the people in your life who drain you dry.

I can see the light of a clear blue morning.
I can see the light of a brand-new day.
I can see the light of a clear blue morning.
And everything's gonna be all right, it's gonna
be okay.

One of the most important lessons I've figured out is that working hard is not just effort—it's learning. It's trying new things, things that interest you that you might be scared to do or think you won't be able to do. Learning more is all about taking chances.

I have taken some mighty big chances in my

life. Some of them have worked out, some haven't. However, every time I have stepped out of my comfort zone, I have learned a ton of valuable lessons—lessons that helped me in all parts of my life.

Almost everybody knows about my decision to leave *The Porter Wagoner Show* back in the 1970s. Lord knows plenty has been said and written about it, so I don't want to walk those steps again. However, it is worth mentioning in terms of describing the process of taking chances.

At the time, Porter was the most successful country artist on television. I'd like to say that I enjoyed every minute of being on his show, but I didn't. Although I certainly enjoyed a lot of it, I just knew that after a while I had to try to make my own way as a solo artist. I wanted to write more, try my hand at movies, and broaden my own musical horizons. I couldn't be happy staying where I was, so I knew I had to leave.

It's easy all these years later to make it sound

like I just said, "See you later," and breezed out the door. It wasn't like that. I was apprehensive and a little scared, but I did not fear failure. I've always had more guts than talent. To me, working without fear is the ultimate freedom. At that time, I thought the very worst that could happen when I left was that I would have to go home. I knew that my family in East Tennessee loved me, and I was already a success in their eyes. But something good always comes from everything. Not only did I learn a lot when I went out on my own, I also wrote "I Will Always Love You" to sing to Porter so he would know my heart and how much I truly did appreciate him. And that I would always love him. I will always love Porter and Whitney Houston for the great success of that song.

The same was true when I started branching out into pop music, and even writing and singing some dance music. People squawked and complained and swore that I had lost my mind, and that I was abandoning country. Some people really wanted me to fail. I didn't listen to any of those people. I never do. I simply chose to toss their negativity onto the express train that ran in one ear and out the other.

I do care about what people think of me and my decisions, as long as they are people who care enough to know who I really am. As far as people who act like they know what is best for me—I know there is no greater expert on me than me.

I really wish you could have seen the looks on my lawyer's and business manager's faces when I told them I wanted to start a theme park in the hills of my hometown in East Tennessee and call it Dollywood. They thought I had already taken the train to Crazywood! Yet I knew it was the right decision for me. And once again, I have learned so much in the process. The creation of Dollywood and Splash Country paved the way for us to launch Dixie Stampede and Pirates Voyage.

As I write this, more than sixty million people have enjoyed our attractions, and that has given us the confidence to continue to expand and grow. None of this would have happened if I had not decided to take a chance all those years ago.

I also learned a lot from being involved in a Broadway musical. I met new people who've already influenced some of my future plans. I studied the Broadway way of doing things, and as a result, I am hoping it will help me when I go back there with other projects.

Learning is all about doing your homework and then taking a chance. The homework part is critical. That means reading (and understanding) feasibility studies, research and hard planning to make sure your ideas make sense. Sometimes it means listening to other experts. It is this studying and thinking through ideas that make projects a true success.

I love being able to do things that create opportunities for others, because that's when you learn

that you've become more than just your success . . .
when you learn you've achieved your dreams and
helped somebody else achieve theirs. So if I have
but one request of you, I ask you to roll up your
sleeves, take a chance and learn more.

Three

CARE MORE

The thing that's always worked for me is the fact that I look so totally artificial, but am so totally real. It gives me something to work against. I have to overcome myself. I have to prove how good I am.

Until I was a teenager, I used red poke-
berries for lipstick and a burnt match-
stick for eyeliner. I used honeysuckle
for perfume. We were raised in the Pentecostal
Church of God and they believed that wearing
makeup was sinful. My Grandpa Jake, my Mama's
dad, was a preacher. So I had to sneak around and
make myself look all pretty but then wash it off
before they caught me.

Once I was in my teens, I traded nature's
makeup for the stuff they sold at the stores. I often

tell the story of how I thought the most beautiful woman in the county was the woman most people called trash. In my eyes—with her big dyed hair, her bright red nails, her feet squeezed tight into her high heel shoes, and all her paint and perfume—she was just perfect. I wanted to look just like her.

Of course, when I would get all dolled up like her, I tried to keep it from my Mama and Grandpa.

Then one day I tripped up and I was busted. Mama saw me in all my painted wonder.

Mama sized me up and the first words out of her mouth were "Do you think you will ever get to heaven looking like that?"

"Of course I wanna go to heaven, Mama," I said, "but I don't think I have to look like hell to get there."

"You look like a trollop," Mama scolded back in her shrill but gruff voice when she felt I'd stepped over the line.

To that I said belligerently, "I don't care!"

She whacked me on the back of my head and jerked me around to face her. "Don't ever let me hear you say you don't care. I didn't put you here on earth to just suck up the air and not care."

The few people in this world who care more change the world and the people around them. Those who don't give a rat's behind have to have someone to care for them.

As I was preparing the UT commencement speech, Mama's words kept coming back to me. My mother had slapped me on the back of my head and imprinted "Care More" in my brain. Now all I had to do was to slap all those graduating kids in the back of their multicolored hairdos and impart a few thoughts that they would remember for a lifetime.

Well, nowadays you can't slap sense into your kids like you could back then. Since I can't tweet or text all of them, I decided to use my best tools to try and motivate them. I would sing and write words, and maybe they would listen.

I learned a long time ago that "telling" or "preaching" to young people—or adults, for that matter—just bounces off their ears like a satellite. They don't catch it; they just deflect it away.

The song that most frequently comes to mind when I think of kids who were not taught to care enough not to hurt other kids' feelings is "The Coat of Many Colors." It's a true story from my childhood and is so personal to me. I cannot tell you how many times someone has walked up to me to tell me how much the song meant to them. Everybody at some time has been ridiculed or devalued or made to feel much less than they really are. It doesn't feel good, because you know you are not what they are making you feel. And sad to say, it's a hurt many people never overcome.

Yet this little song, because it deals with something everyone has felt, seems to have a healing effect on people. I receive letters and e-mails from teachers all over the country who tell me they use the song as a way to address bullying and respecting the differences in all of us. Sometimes they simply sing the song and discuss it. Other times, the children make their own coats with construction paper, each square representing something in their lives. It really touches my heart to think that the song is being used to teach respect and tolerance. I'm proud that in a small way my little song has helped so many people.

Back through the years I go wanderin' once
*   again,*
Back to the seasons of my youth.
I recall a box of rags someone gave us
And how my Mama put those rags
*   to use.*
There were rags of many colors, but every
*   piece was small.*
I didn't have a coat and it was way down in
*   the fall.*

Mama sewed the rags together, sewin' every
    piece with love.
She made my Coat of Many Colors that I was
    so proud of.
While Mama sewed she told a story from the
    Bible she had read
About a Coat of Many Colors Joseph wore and
    then she said,
"I hope this coat will bring you good luck and
    happiness."
And I just couldn't wait to wear it,
And Mama blessed it with a kiss.

My Coat of Many Colors that my Mama
    made for me,
Made only from rags, but I wore it so
    proudly
And although we had no money, I was rich as
    I could be
In my Coat of Many Colors, Mama made
    for me.

Care More

So with patches on my britches, holes in both
  my shoes,
In my Coat of Many Colors I hurried off to
  school
Just to find the others laughin' and makin' fun
  of me
And my Coat of Many Colors that Mama
  made for me.

And, oh, I couldn't understand that, cause I
  felt I was rich
And I told them of the love that Mama sewed
  in every stitch.
I even told them all that story
That Mama told me while she sewed
And why my Coat of Many Colors
Was worth more than all their clothes.

They didn't understand it and I tried to make
  them see
One is only poor only if they choose to be.

It's true we had no money but I was rich as
I could be
In my Coat of Many Colors, Mama made
for me.

This refusal to judge has been important in my life in other ways, as well. My Mama had a good understanding of me, in spite of our early makeup encounter, so she knew I was a good girl. She even once sewed some shoulder pads from a jacket into my bra to give me a little push-up after I had started performing as a teenager. (That was before I discovered Frederick's of Hollywood.) I learned a lot about understanding and acceptance from my Mama because at a time when people totally misunderstood me, she knew exactly what I was all about.

I have received hundreds of offers to judge songwriting, contests, television shows, beauty pageants, drag queen shows. . . . Heck, I have even been asked to judge dog shows! So far I've turned them all down. It's just hard for me to tell someone they are better than everyone else—or perhaps better said, to tell someone they are not as good as someone else.

I remember on Christmas and sometimes other special holidays, some of our churches would bring baskets of food and occasionally clothes and even toys to our family. I remember that we were excited to get it, on one hand. On the other, we knew we were getting it because they judged us as "poor." Well, poor we were, but somehow it made me feel less than other kids.

When we created the Imagination Library, I made sure that every child in the area who signed up received the books. I never want a child to have that feeling that somehow they are less than someone else—or more than someone else. Don't judge them by the cover, because they are real good books.

Although I am pretty sure that if no one knew who I was, and you put my picture in front of ten people and asked them how many times this person has been married, I think on the low end, the guess would be two and on the upper end, at least five times. Actually, even knowing who I am, people are surprised to find out that I have been married to the same man for forty-six years. I look like a serial bride, but I am a "one and done" kind of girl.

Next to the ones about cosmetic surgery, the questions most often asked of me are: Why doesn't Carl ever appear anywhere? And what is the secret to your marriage? It certainly makes great fodder for humor, but the truth is, it is about one thing: commitment.

I take commitment very seriously. You find its importance to me in every aspect of my life, but where it is most important to me is in my relationship with Carl. Like everyone else, we have our ups and downs, but we have always been and will always be committed to our love for each other. I do not easily cut and run. If something is broken, then let's fix it. If it's wrong, then let's make it right. This is just my nature—some call it commitment, but it just as easily can be called stubbornness!

I do think much of what makes a relationship work well is the same as what makes a partnership successful. I have been blessed to have several people in my life who not only have been fabulous people to work with but also remain my closest friends.

Judy Ogle and Don Warden have been with me every step of the way. Judy was my best friend in elementary school and she remains my best friend today. Judy works for me and with me. By "for me," all I mean is that I provide her a paycheck. The much more important part is that she has worked with me over the entire arc of my life. We have rarely had a disagreement about work, because she does not want to disappoint me and I do not want to disappoint her.

Don's been working with me for more than

forty years. He is not a tall man, but I have looked up to him ever since we met on *The Porter Wagoner Show.*

Teresa Hughes and Richard Dennison, my left and right hands, have been in my working family more years than we can count. They do whatever needs to be done, so rest assured they have done just about everything.

The new guy on the team is Ted Miller, who helped me launch Dollywood, Dixie Stampede, Pirates Voyage, the Dollywood Foundation and the Imagination Library. He has been there for me in so many ways, both in business and personally, for more than twenty-seven years. He comes off probation in a year or two, so I reckon he has made it now as a full-time employee!

And, of course, my precious Uncle Bill, who has guided my career my whole life.

Am I lucky? You bet. But I also think success has a lot to do with commitment. They are committed to me, and I am committed to them. It also has a great deal to do with the wisdom of deciding just to whom you are committing.

I know lots of people who I like so much but would never choose to hire. They may be funny or crazy and a ball to be around, but those same traits may not be very useful in a work environment. "Funny and crazy" may also mean inconsistent, undependable and erratic—and those qualities just drive me up a wall.

When I examine both my personal and professional lives through the lens of my friendships and coworkers, it is pretty clear to me why they have worked so well.

First and foremost is dead-on, wide-eyed, blunt, total, transparent honesty. It's the way I am wired, so I know I will always be honest, and I expect the same thing in return. Though we might not want to talk about a problem, if it needs to be said, then we say it. I find this to be a rare commodity in the world. Some people seem more comfortable with deception than they are with truth. And some are so concerned about what you might think of them, they want to tell you what they think you want to hear. This is dangerous territory.

Carl doesn't like my version of "Stairway to Heaven." Judy will tell me if I am showing more cleavage than the situation calls for. Ted will talk about the aftermath of my passing to the great beyond. I really don't want to hear any of this, but it all needs to be said to me. I care what they think— be it good or bad. If I valued dishonesty, Carl would tell me my version is much better than Led Zeppelin's. Judy would tell me how all the kids love my cleavage. And Ted would just say, "We will figure all that out after you die."

I also have to be honest about myself. In my kind of business, it is very easy to get too big for your britches. An inflated ego is dangerous, because it seduces you into thinking you know everything about everything. I know there is a lot I don't know and there are lots of folks who are much more talented than I am. So I focus on what I do best and remain clear on the things I do not know about, so I can go out and find the right person who does.

For instance, I do not know much about running Dollywood and Dixie Stampede on a daily basis. I don't even want to know about that. I do know our shared vision of bringing family entertainment to the Smokies. I do know a thing or two about writing and producing our shows. And I sure know how to promote them. The success of both Dollywood and Dixie Stampede comes from our ability to each work in the areas of our expertise. Because, believe me, if I were in charge of the daily operation, I know I would give away far too many tickets and, certainly, colas and ice cream to all the kids!

The first place I look when I am choosing to work with someone is at his or her eyes. If it's a man and he is looking at my eyes, then I think he is looking for my intelligence. If he looks at my mouth, then I know he is looking for my wit. But if he's not looking where everyone else looks first, then he may be looking for a man!

I do realize I have to give the guys a few minutes to adjust before they look at my eyes.

Seriously, I first look for trust in someone. Trust usually builds over time and is more often than not built by consistently keeping all the small commitments. Work on a daily basis is all about small commitments. One pet peeve I have is punctuality. To me, being on time is keeping a small commitment.

Over and over again, keeping these small commitments adds up to trust. If people cannot consistently fulfill their small commitments, then they sure cannot consistently keep the big ones.

Next for me is that trust leads to respect. I love the old saying "When respect is gone, the biggest part of love dies." I think this is true for relationships and partnerships. Respect is confidence that the job will be done and will be done right, but it

is also about how the job will be done. I have never
believed in a scorched-earth policy of achieving
your goals, meaning I do not feel that the end jus-
tifies the means. I've always said I will step over
you or around you to get where I am going, but I
will never step on you.

Finally, all this leads to love and caring. I truly
love all my closest colleagues, because I trust them
and respect them. These folks feel like my family.
I will do anything for them, and they will do
anything for me. I feel their joy, and I hurt with
their hurts. It's a powerful emotional connection
that may not be advised in the latest management
books, but it works for me. I care more for my
people than most employers probably do, and they
take care of me.

This is not to say that it is all perfect. I believe
everyone in my life was placed there by God.
There are people that I truly respect and love, but
who also drive me crazy. They can be difficult,
obstinate and narrow-minded. Yet I learn from

these things, too. Their behavior may reveal something to me that I have forgotten or point out something that's missing in me.

I hang on to the robe, because my belief in God is so strong that I truly do not believe that anybody is a mistake. People like to say, when someone is giving you trouble, even in your own house, that the devil is at work. I never believe it. It's always God at work, because God puts the challenging people there for me, to care about them and to learn from them.

So if I have one favor to ask you, it is to care more. Leave the judging to God.

Four

BE MORE

Plan your life and do what you do best. You can be absolutely anything you want to be. You may not want to be a star, but you do want to star in your own dreams.

I try to always remember where I came from, who I am and why I wanted to do this to start with. It was not to get away from my family. It was not because I wasn't proud of my home that I wanted to leave it. I just wanted to take the Smoky Mountains wherever I went.

I wanna run like a cheetah, roar like a lion.
Soar like an eagle, even when I'm scared of
flyin'.
I wanna fight like a tiger, be as gentle as a
lamb.
I wanna be somebody, proud of who I am.

When I was seven or eight years old, after a visit from our doctor, Robert F. Thomas, I heard Daddy say when he left, "He is a real somebody."

For the longest time, I kept rolling that around in my small brain. Yes, he is real, and, yes, he is somebody. . . . He is Dr. Robert Thomas!

Now as I reflect on what Daddy was trying to say, it is crystal clear. He was putting the emphasis on "real." He clearly understood the difference between someone who was self-important or famous and someone who was authentic. When my Daddy died, I vowed that I would truly work at being a real somebody.

I served for more than thirty years as the Honorary Chairperson for the Dr. Robert F. Thomas Foundation in my home community. Long ago I accepted the role because I knew I could raise more money than most or donate it to help the foundation bring high-quality health care to our area. I want my family, our employees and all my friends and neighbors to have access to the best medical care around. It is important to me that the women in our area have their babies and seek treatment from good doctors in good facilities. And who knows—maybe one day we will have the greatest spa in the world here. After all, good care doesn't happen just when you are sick. We need to look good and feel good to be good!

I do what I have done for the Thomas Foundation because Dr. Thomas helped me into the world, so I have an affinity for him and for his vision. I know I get a lot more credit for things than I actually deserve, but over time, this honor has made me be more than I otherwise would have been to all the folks in my hometown.

My point is, if you care enough to tackle important responsibilities that help others, then you become a better person. Besides, since my Daddy thought Dr. Thomas was a real somebody, I know he would be proud of me.

Many people have a daily commitment to exercise because it makes them feel better—more alive, more alert and more excited about the world. I get these same feelings from prayer.

When I was young, I often heard the passage from scripture, "Pray without ceasing." It always stuck with me. Back then I thought, *How in the world can you pray without ceasing?* I now know what that means. I feel the ever-presence that God is always right there with me . . . to listen to my questions and guide me to always strive to be more.

To me, there is a great irony to "be more," and it is actually to be less. To be more makes me be less apt to judge . . . to be less apt to make excuses for my own behavior, and to be less apt to be self-serving and self-righteous.

Now, my purpose here is not to preach to you (although I think I would make a pretty good preacher, praise the Lord), but what I mean by "being less" is for you to place yourself in God's trust.

I always call that spiritual center that we all have inside us my "God core." I think of it as the place in everybody where heaven and earth kind of meet. I have always tried to listen to that God core in me, and it's never steered me wrong.

Sometimes I can fool myself and think I am so smart and so talented and I've got things all figured out, but that only lasts a little while. For me to really be more, I have to stop, pray and ask for God's guidance to help me see things more clearly. To do that, I need quiet and solitude. I am most open to hearing God in the early morning—long before sunrise. It is a ritual for me, a daily routine to offer up my earthly concerns to receive heavenly advice and comfort. Sometimes it takes a while to understand what I'm supposed to do, and sometimes the guidance is revealed in strange and mysterious ways.

Since that day I gave the speech at UT, I have had numerous requests to write a book—this book—and give more speeches. Well, first and foremost, I am an entertainer. Now, after fifty years, that comes fairly naturally. Writing a book and giving speeches—those are harder than fitting into a tight girdle!

Two of my associates, Ted Miller and David Dotson, challenged me in front of the Dollywood Foundation board members to go ahead and write this book. It kind of upset me and confused me at the same time, because we had not discussed this project before the meeting and their behavior was totally out of character for both of them. It felt like they were putting pressure on me to do what they wanted me to do.

Early the next morning, I was sitting in my bed on my bus, trying to sort out why this bothered me so much. Then it came to me as clear as it could be. My irritation with them was more about my own irritation with myself. I had talked about writing this book for some time, but I just kept pushing it to the background, because I did not feel it was the right time. The fact that they acted out of character was really the push I needed to get off the fence—my fence—and decide to get into gear and stop talking and start doing. Once I figured this out, things got back on track.

We talked about it later, and they assured me they were certainly not trying to manipulate me or the situation. They were just excited by the project, and they believed in me. It was the sign I was looking for . . . a sign I call my God clue.

I am very fortunate to live with my own personal fountain of God clues: my husband, Carl. I cannot tell you how many times I have been sitting at home stewing over some decision I have to make. Carl will be over on the couch, seemingly oblivious to everything I am thinking. Then out of nowhere he will say something, and I'll get all wide-eyed and say, "What did you say?" So many times it will be exactly what I need to hear. What he has said has nothing specific to do with what I am thinking, but by saying what is on his mind, and by being true and honest, he gives me the answers I need.

This is how I look for my answers. My experience has been that God doesn't set too many bushes on fire in front of you, nor does some booming voice come from high above to tell me what to do. I'm no Abraham or Moses. But I've learned over the years that if I work on my relationship with God and I reach deep inside myself and focus on my daily prayer, then I know where I should look for my answers. So, I go from not having a clue to discovering my God clue.

I am a seeker, a poor sinful creature;
There is no weaker than I am.
I am a seeker, you are a teacher;
You are a reacher so reach down,
Reach out and lead me, guide me and keep me
In the shelter of your care each day.
'Cause I am a seeker, but you are a keeper;
You are the leader, won't you show me the way.

I am certainly no angel. But for better or worse, people have always found me to be someone who can help them, inspire them, comfort them and console them. My friends all call me the Dolly-Mama. I have often been asked what it is about me that seems to conjure up these feelings in other people. My mother was like that. She, too, loved everybody.

I believe that people are drawn and healed by a positive energy. There is an energy to everything, both positive and negative. Love is about the best energy there can be. I always ask God to let me shine with his love and with his light. I am always looking for that light. I am always working toward that light. And I am always working with that light and in that light.

People need confidence and when they see confidence in other people, they try to get close to it. It's only natural.

I know I am no fairy godmother with a magic wand that can solve every problem. It's been my experience that there is a very thin line between arrogance and confidence. I think the difference between the two is humility.

I never consider myself a superstar, because I know myself too well. I am not better than anyone else, but I do know that I try each day to try a little harder. That's my confidence.

Confidence, everybody shout it.
Confidence, what ya gonna do without it?
Confidence, we've gotta build our confidence.

And if you ain't got it, dig down and get it.
If you've got a problem, come on and admit it.
We're gonna work on it, so everybody hit it.
Let's work on confidence.

It's easy to look like me. All you need is a stuffed shirt, wigs, high heels and makeup. I describe my look as a blend of Mother Goose, Cinderella and the local hooker. In fact, there're a lot of drag queens and Dolly look-alikes, and there are a lot of Dolly look-alike contests. I even entered one once—and lost! I know that I'm known for my physical attributes, but I know the real me is in my heart and in my actions. And the real you resides in your heart and your actions.

Some of the toughest requests of celebrities come from the Make-A-Wish Foundation and other organizations that are dedicated to making the wishes of terminally ill and disabled children come true. I say "toughest" because one feels every emotion—sad about a child's struggles, mad about their suffering and glad that one can be just a tiny bit of comfort to them.

As I grow older, I have come to realize that by taking a few minutes to simply hold hands, sing and laugh with a child who has a terminal condition, I am being given a gift that is indescribable when they smile and say thank you. I should be thanking them for making my heart bigger. They are the inspiration, not me.

My faith, most certainly, has something to do with my upbringing. When you are poor and live in the country, you have to believe. For example, you have to believe your sick brother will get well. You can't afford a doctor or medicine, so all you really have is faith that he'll get better. If you are struggling and not sure where your next meal will come from, the only comfort to your uncertainty is your faith that somehow, some way, that next meal will be provided to you.

Circumstances like these nurtured my faith rather than destroyed it. It brought me closer to

God, which, in turn, has given me more confidence, more energy and more faith.

While I am comfortable with my spirituality, I want you to understand that this in no way means I think I have something no one else possesses. Being comfortable with my spirituality means I accept the fact that I often stumble and stray off the path. Yet I know the path I have chosen, and I know everybody can choose to walk in God's light in their own way. One thing is for certain—I would believe in God even if there wasn't one!

All my life I have walked a fine line. I'm too bad to be good and too good to be bad. I also walk a fine line between being gaudy and sexy. My spirituality and my sensuality seem to be intertwined. But I'm too cartoonish to ever be a threat to wives and girlfriends. Not to say I might or might not have ever crossed the line. Even Snow White slept with seven dwarfs!

I know through my own life experiences that I am like every other woman I know. I have been fat, so I know how hard it is to lose weight. I have been wrinkled and had it fixed. I have looked up at a glass ceiling, and thrown one of my five-inch high heels and smashed right through it. I understand why women need to look their best, and I am no different. I have learned to cook and take great pride in my recipes.

Over the years, I have seen some fun T-shirts and bumper stickers that say "Dolly for Governor," or even "Dolly for President." Naturally, I know these are in jest and come from some of my fans. It makes me stop and think about how fortunate I am. I do not want to be governor or president. . . . I just want to be the best Dolly Parton I can be.

I think that in the end people remember us for who we are—not what we look like, how many records we sell or how much money we make. As I've said before, my blessings are many. I have a loving family and wonderful friends. I love my job. I have a great hometown. And I live in the best state in the USA and in the best country in the whole wide world.

So what does it mean to be more? Is it measured by how many hits I have or the number of awards that I've been given? Of course not. Being more is all about following the Golden Rule and bringing into your life a commitment to be fair, generous and compassionate to everybody. And I do mean *everybody*! So if I have but one hope for you—always remember you cannot be more than a real somebody!

ONE MORE THING . . .

Over the years, I have had a few angels in my life. I have mentioned several in this book. These angels have helped me succeed, taught me things I needed to understand to grow, and returned my love.

Together we have Dreamed More, Learned More, Cared More and Become More.

One of those angels is Carl Dean, who just told me to turn out the light and quit wiggling the bed. And when I hear good advice from angels, I pay attention to it. So . . . good night!

Love
Dolly

I'll bet we'll see each other again in a movie, or
hear each other in a song or just meet up on the
road of life. But if you're still not finished reading,
here are a few little goodies that I hope you enjoy,
and that might bring a smile to your lips and lift
your spirits.

P.S.

Because I believe in you and know that you can do anything you set your mind to, here are the lyrics to the song "Try" that I sung at the UT graduation. The feelings in it mean a lot to me, and maybe they will to you, too.

*I've chased after rainbows; I have captured one
   or two.*
*I've reached for the stars; and I've even held
   a few.*
*I've walked that lonesome valley, topped the
   mountains, soared the sky.*
*I've laughed and I have cried; but I have
   always tried.*

*I've always been a dreamer, and dreams are
   special things.*
*But dreams are of no value if they're not
   equipped with wings.*
*Secure yourself for climbing, make ready for
   the sky.*
*Don't let your chance go by; you'll make it if
   you try.*

Try to be the first one up the mountain,
The highest-flying dreamer in the sky.

Try your best to be an inspiration
For others that are still afraid and shy.
Try to make the most of every moment.
If you fail, get up and try again.
Try each day a little harder.
If you never try you never win.

Nothing is impossible if you can just believe.
Don't live your life in shackles when faith can
    be your key.
The winner's one who keeps determination in
    his eyes.
Who's not afraid to fly and not afraid to try.

Try to be the first one up the mountain.
Try to be the first to touch the sky.
Don't let somebody tell you you can't do it.
If they do, then show them it's a lie.
If you fail at first, just keep on trying.
You are not a failure in God's eyes.

*The path you're taking now can make a
    difference.*
It all depends on just how hard you try.

The first step is always the hardest.
But nothing's gonna change if you don't try.

*So spread your wings and let the magic
    happen.*
You'll never really know unless you try.

THE WIT AND WISDOM OF THE DOLLY-MAMA

I've said a lot of things along the way that people remember, and they've said I should include them in a book. Well here I go.

I'm not going to limit myself just because people won't accept the fact that I can do something else.

. . .

I never let a rhinestone go unturned.

. . .

The way I look is just a country girl's idea of glam.

. . .

You'd be surprised how much it costs to make a person look this cheap.

. . .

It's a good thing I was born a girl; otherwise I'd be a drag queen.

. . .

Mama had twelve kids. She had one on her and one in her for as long as I can remember. But we always kept Mama on a pedestal. We kind of had to. That's about the only way we could keep Daddy away from her.

. . .

I can just see two big mountains growing up out of my grave, and people going around on mule rides to look at them.

. . .

I'll take a sandwich and a shake over a joint and a jug anytime.

. . .

My feet are small for the same reason my waist is small—things don't grow in the shade.

. . .

I think of country radio like a great lover. You were great to me, you bought me a lot of nice things and then you dumped my ass for younger women.

. . .

I have no taste and no style and nobody cares. I love it!

. . .

If it hadn't been for music, I'd have been a beautician. Even if I wasn't in show business, I would have wanted to be glamorous—and that's about the only way a girl in a small Southern town is going to get it. Or maybe I'd have been a missionary; I've thought about that, too, but where would I get my hair done?

. . .

I can tell you where to put it if I don't like where you've got it.

. . .

God and I have a great relationship, but we both see other people.

. . .

I look at myself like a show dog. I've got to keep her clipped and trimmed and in good shape.

. . .

I'm just the girl next door, provided you live next door to a circus.

. . .

I'm not ever going to have a wardrobe malfunction, because I'd probably take out the first three rows.

. . .

I like to buy clothes that are two sizes too small and then take them in a little.

. . .

Plastic surgeons are always making mountains out of molehills.

. . .

I always say, if I see something sagging, dragging or bagging, I'm gonna have it nipped, sucked, tucked or plucked.

. . .

Home is where I hang my hair.

. . .

I owe a lot of folks a lot of thanks, but I give the praise and honor to God for whatever talent and good luck that I've had. God gets the credit; I get the cash!

. . .

Back there in the hills, my folks loved each other and they loved us. But people ask me, "How in the world, living in a small house like that with twelve kids, did you have any privacy?" I say, "Well, we had a wash pan. And we washed down as far as possible, and then we washed up as far as possible; and when everybody cleared the room, we washed possible."

. . .

I had to get rich so I could afford to sing like I was poor again.

. . .

I always try to read the tabloids so I can see what I'm up to now. I believe everything about everybody but me.

THE TRUTH,
DOLLY STYLE

I've been asked a lot of questions over the years—
sometimes the same questions over and over. Here
are some of the classic questions, with my shoot-
from-the-hip answers.

Are they real?

*Of course not. I could never grow my nails this
long.*

How long does it take to do your hair?
I don't really know. I'm never there.

What do you want people to say about you one hundred years from now?
Boy, don't she look good for her age.

What is your favorite color?
Miss Clairol #289.

Would you ever run for president?
Lord, no. Don't you think we've had enough boobs in the White House?

Is it true you met your husband at the Wishy-Washy Laundromat?
Yes, it's true, and it's been wishy-washy ever since.

How has your marriage survived for more than forty years?

I stay gone.

Do you ever get tired of dumb-blonde jokes?

No, 'cause I know I'm not dumb, and I know I'm not blond.

Is it true a rich oil sheik offered you a million dollars to spend a weekend with him on his private island?

Before I answer that, could you just give me a minute to shake the sand out of my drawers.

How do you play so many instruments with those long nails?

Pretty good, if I do say so myself.

You are one of twelve children—you must be Catholic.

No, we aren't Catholic. We are just a bunch of horny hillbillies. You know my family was big on the three Rs—reading, writing and reproduction.

If you could have starred in any movie, which one would you have been in?

The Silence of the Lambs—*where Anthony Hopkins played Hannibal Lecter, that creepy old man that ate everybody. We could have called it* Dinner at Hooters!

I'm sure you have man after man approach you. How do you handle temptation?

I don't.

A plastic surgeon was quoted in the tabloids as saying you'd had plastic surgery. Is it true?

No, I was born with my eyebrows on top of my head.

Is it hard to stay in touch with your roots?

No. I have them touched up every two weeks.

How does it feel to be Dr. Dolly?

I love being Dr. Dolly, and one thing is for sure—when people call me a Double-D now, it has a whole new meaning.

Do you have a stimulus package?

Ask my husband.

What is the worst thing your husband ever said to you?

"I do!"

Do you suffer from PMS?

Does that stand for pretty miserable stuff? The director of Steel Magnolias' *greatest fear was that all of us women would have PMS at the same time.*

How tall are you?

Five-one, but with heels six-two.

Were you ever involved in the women's liberation movement in the 1970s?

Yes, as a matter of fact, I burned my bra. It took the Nashville Fire Department three days to put out the fire. Some say it's still burning.

Have you ever cheated on your husband?

*Yes, once, when we were playing Monopoly.
(Did I get out of that one good?)*

If you could change anything about yourself,
what would it be?

These shoes I've got on . . . they are killing me.

Will there ever be a *Best Little Whorehouse 2*?

*There will always be a Whorehouse somewhere,
but I won't always be in it.*

Have you ever had a voice lesson?

*Good Lord, no. Why in the world would you teach
somebody to sound like this?*

How do you look without your hair and makeup?

Like hammered snot.

What is your best physical feature?

Actually I have two . . . my eyes and my smile. Well, actually, that's three; but I know what you were thinking.

My twins have been great to me. I don't know if I'm supporting them or if they're supporting me.

Describe your perfect date.

That would be April 25. It's not too hot, not too cold and you only need a light jacket.

Does it bother you being so short?

No, I'd be tall if I hadn't gotten so bunched up at top.

Do you look more like your mother or father?

That depends on whether or not I'm wearing makeup.

ACKNOWLEDGMENTS

My personal thanks to:

Ted Miller

David Dotson

Judy Ogle

Don Warden

Bryan Seaver

Tim Rauhoff

Teresa Hughes

Richard Dennison

Rachel George and crew

Cassie Parton and crew

Acknowledgments

Steve Summers

Cheryl Riddle

Danny Nozell and CTK

Mary Lyda Wellons

Terry Garrison

Paul Couch

Buddy Sheffield

Susie Glickman

Pat Resnick

Jane Wagner

Buzz Cohen

David Phillips

Louis Owens

Bill Owens

Porter Wagoner and family

My entire family

The Herschend family

My musical family

My Dollywood and Splash Country Family

Fred Hardwick and my Dixie Stampede family, especially Bill Lloyd Sr., who believed in the Imagination

Acknowledgments

Library as much as I did and is now launching the program in heaven.

Special thanks to the Dollywood Foundation and Imagination Library board of directors and staff, and to all of the kind and generous sponsors who make the Imagination Library a reality for their children:

Jeff Conyers
Doreen McCammon
Sherry French
Kate Phillips
Karen Wilson
Pam Moser Hunsaker
Christy Crouse
Ken Bell
Barbara Joines
Charles Kite
Ann Warden
Jo Blalock
Edna Rogers
Gord Kretz

Acknowledgments

Dave Edwards

Wilfred Wilkinson

Catriona Sturton

Roger Stone

Natalie Turnbull

Lisa Vitelli at Penguin Group (USA) Inc.

Finally, many thanks to Ivan Held and Jake Morrissey (a.k.a. Mr. Redletter) at G. P. Putnam's Sons for their commitment to this little book.